Firsts and Seconds

AN INTRODUCTION
TO TWO-PART SINGING

William Appleby
and
Frederick Fowler

OXFORD UNIVERSITY PRESS
MUSIC DEPARTMENT WALTON STREET OXFORD OX2 6DP

LIST OF SONGS

1. Tallis's Canon
2. The Cuckoo *(traditional)*
3. All who sing, and wish to please *(T. Goodban)*
4. The hart he loves the high wood *(traditional)*
5. Now we are met *(T. Goodban)*
6. Haste thee, nymph *(Samuel Arnold)*
7. The Sandman *(German folk-tune, arr. Brahms)*
8. Blow the wind southerly *(Northumbrian folksong)*
9. The Miller's Flowers *(Schubert)*
10. Susanni *(Old German tune, arr. Fritz Jöde)*
11. The Shepherd *(Harry Brook)*
12. Song of the Spirits (from 'Armide') *(Gluck)*
13. O wha's for Scotland, and Charlie?
    (Jacobite song, arr. Herbert Horrocks)
14. Sweet Kate *(Robert Jones)*
15. Summer (from 'Alcina') *(Handel)*
16. How merrily we live *(Michael Este)*
17. The Loadstars *(William Shield)*
18. Ho-la-hi *(German folksong, arr. Roger Fiske)*
19. Song of Farewell *(Austrian folksong, arr. Ferdinand Rauter)*
20. Li'l David, play on yo' harp
    (Negro spiritual, arr. Sebastian H. Brown)
21. Cielito Lindo *(Mexican folk-tune, arr. Phyllis Tate)*

FIRSTS AND SECONDS

1. Tallis's Canon

Words by
Bishop Ken (1637-1711)

Thomas Tallis
(c. 1505-1585)

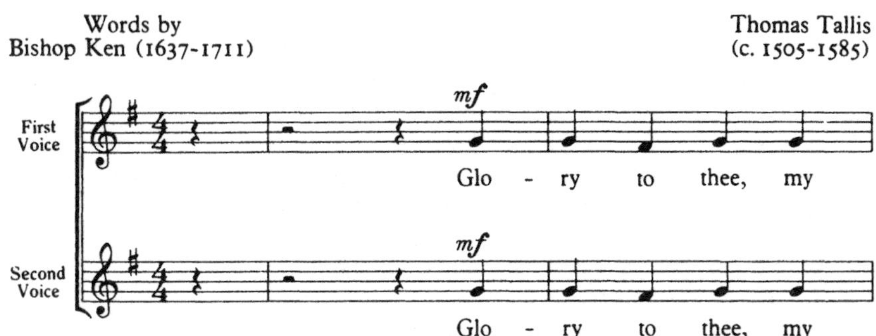

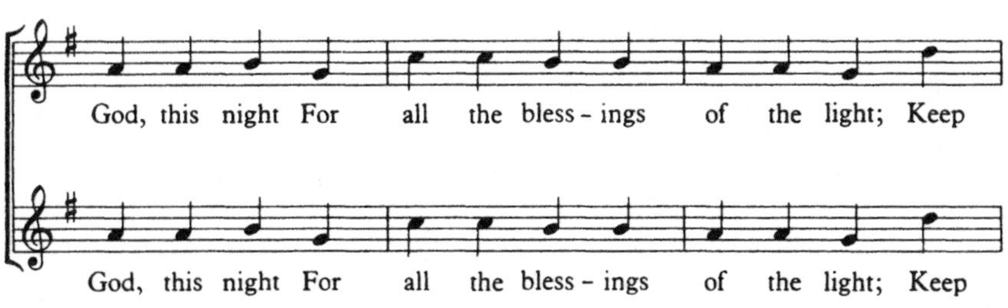

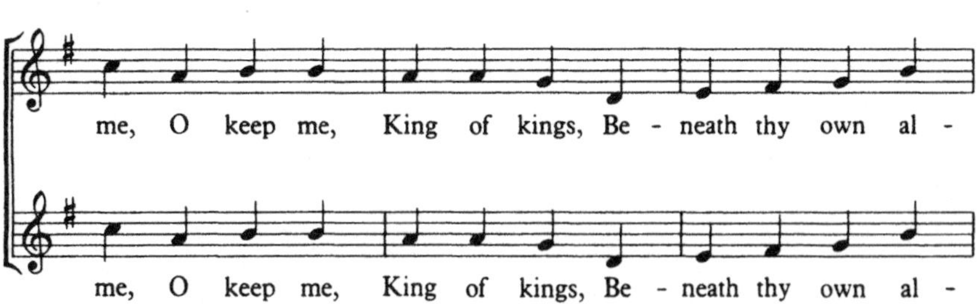

OXFORD UNIVERSITY PRESS, MUSIC DEPARTMENT, WALTON STREET, OXFORD OX2 6DP

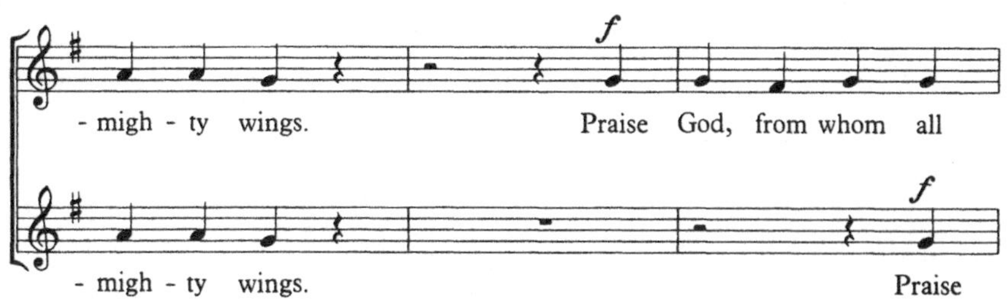
f
- migh - ty wings.
Praise God, from whom all
f
- migh - ty wings.
Praise

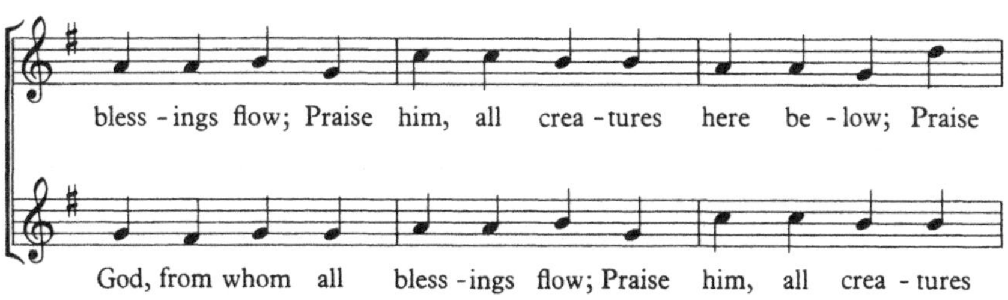
bless - ings flow; Praise him, all crea - tures here be - low; Praise
God, from whom all bless - ings flow; Praise him, all crea - tures

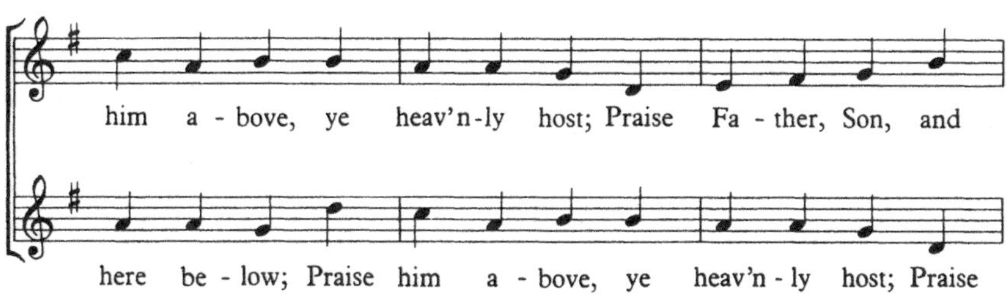
him a - bove, ye heav'n-ly host; Praise Fa - ther, Son, and
here be - low; Praise him a - bove, ye heav'n - ly host; Praise

Ho - ly Ghost.
A - men.
Fa - ther, Son, and Ho - ly Ghost.
A - men.

2. The Cuckoo

Words by
Jacqueline Froom

Traditional

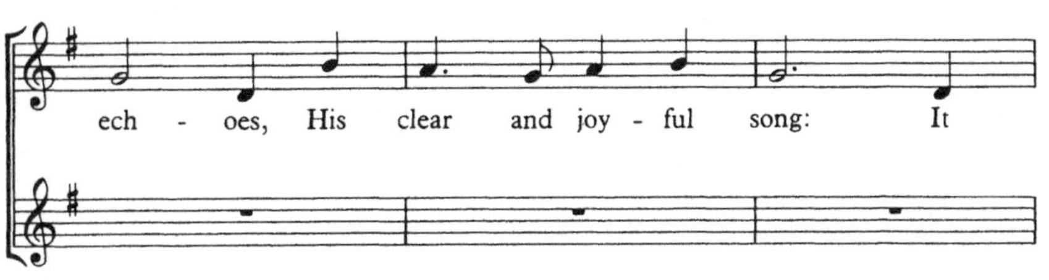

main. "Cuc - koo, cuc - koo, the
song: It rings a - cross the val - ley In

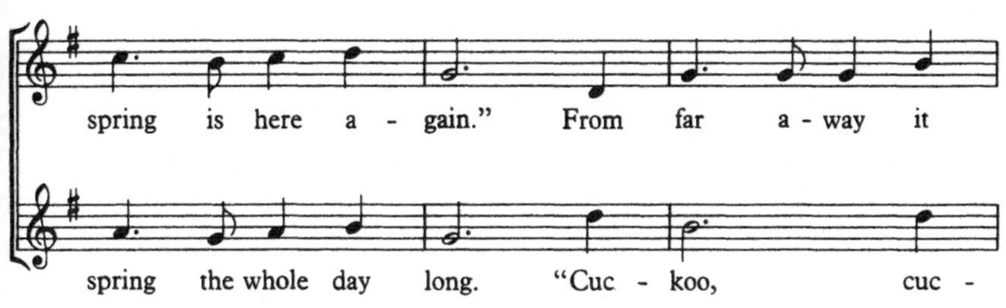
spring is here a - gain." From far a - way it
spring the whole day long. "Cuc - koo, cuc -

ech - oes, His clear and joy - ful song: It
- koo," he sings with might and main. "Cuc -

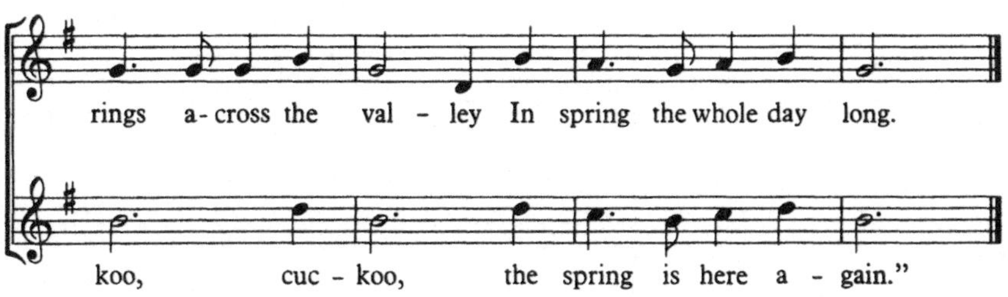
rings a- cross the val - ley In spring the whole day long.
koo, cuc - koo, the spring is here a - gain."

3. All who sing, and wish to please

T. Goodban
(1784-1863)

4. The hart he loves the high wood

Traditional

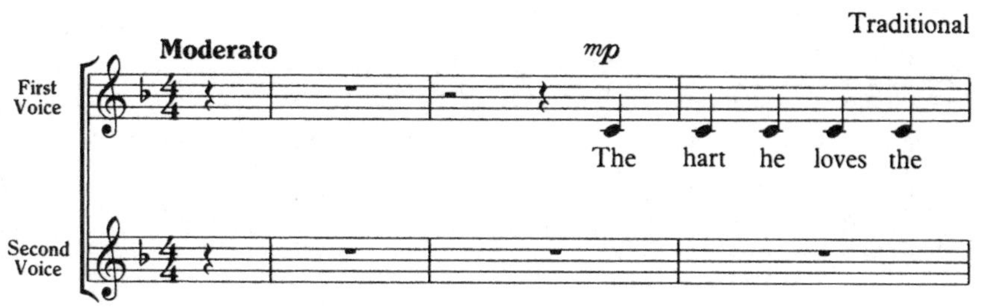

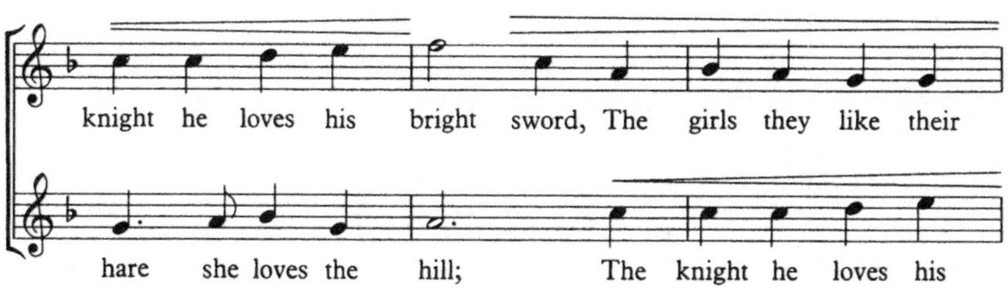

5. Now we are met

T. Goodban
(1784-1863)

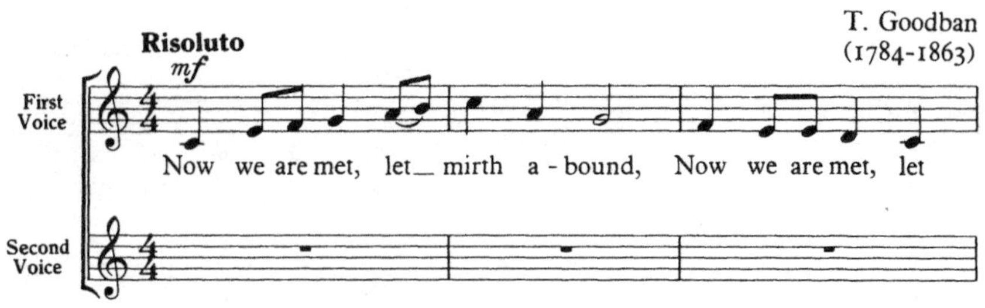

6. Haste thee, nymph

Words by John Milton

Samuel Arnold (1740-1802)

7. The Sandman

Words by
Frances B. Wood

German folk-tune
arranged by Brahms

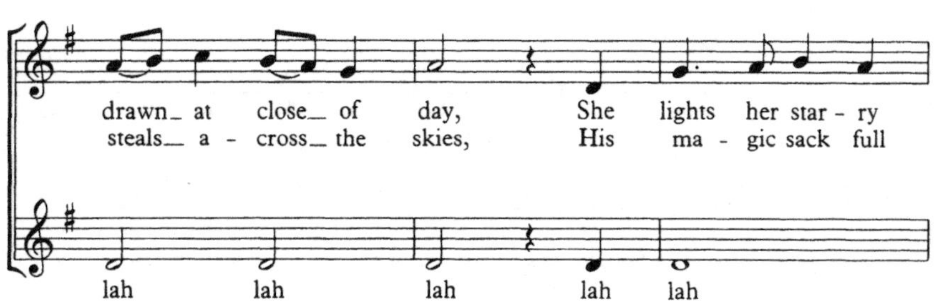

Note: the second voice part has been added by the editors. The words are reprinted by permission.

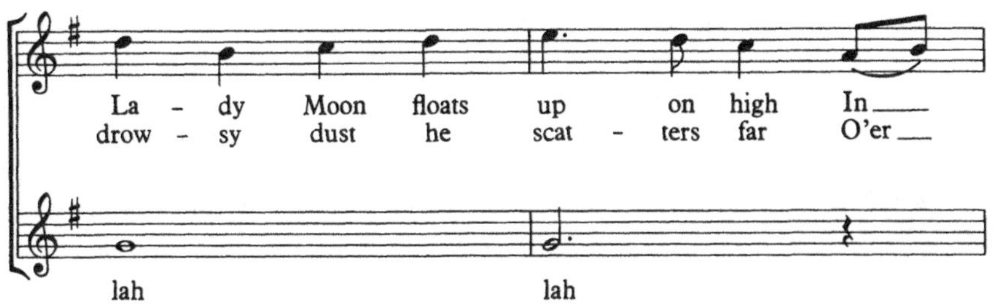
La - dy Moon floats up on high In
drow - sy dust he scat - ters far O'er
lah
lah

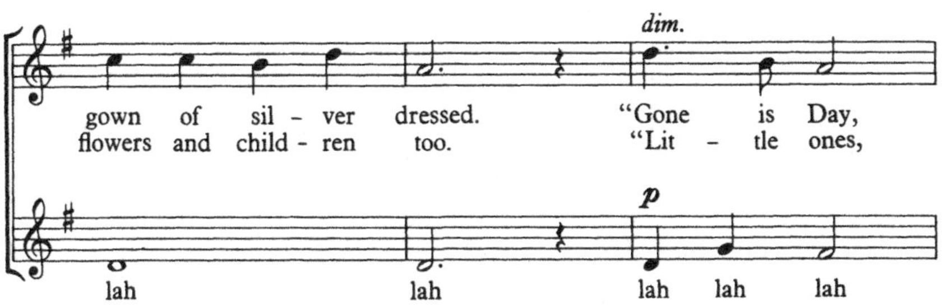
dim.
gown of sil - ver dressed. "Gone is Day,
flowers and child - ren too. "Lit - tle ones,
p
lah
lah
lah lah lah

Time" they say, "For the bu - sy world to
Pret - ty ones Now sleep the long night
lah lah lah lah lah lah lah

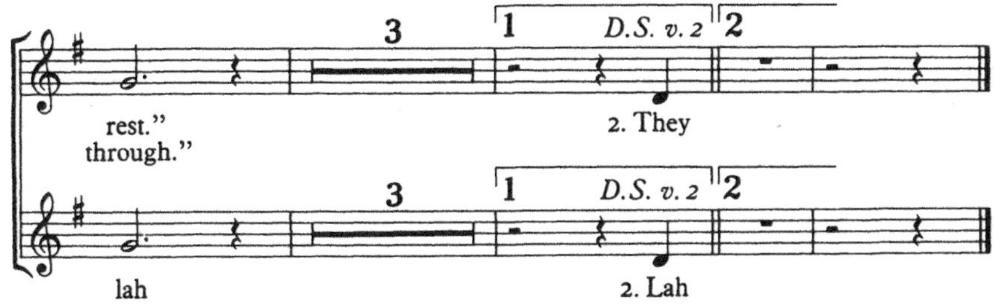
3
1
D.S. v. 2
2
rest."
through."
2. They
lah
2. Lah

8. Blow the wind southerly

Northumbrian folk-song

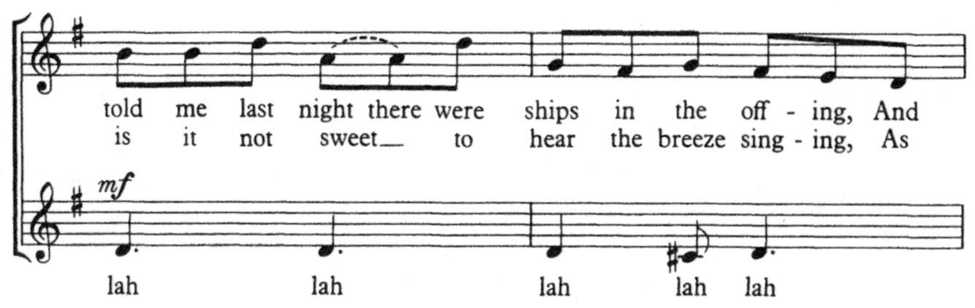
told me last night there were ships in the off - ing, And
is it not sweet to hear the breeze sing - ing, As
mf
lah lah lah lah lah

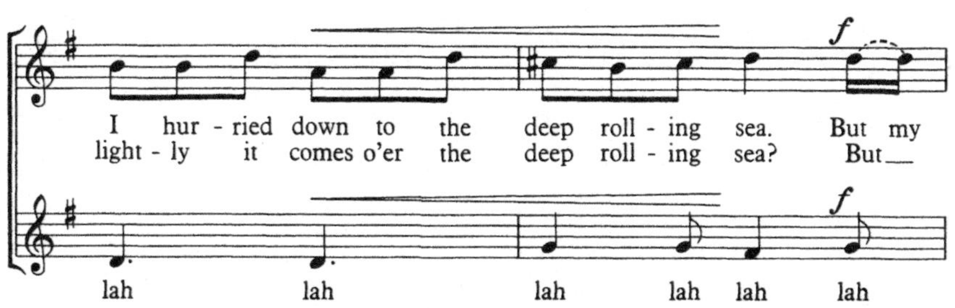
f
I hur - ried down to the deep roll - ing sea. But my
light - ly it comes o'er the deep roll - ing sea? But
f
lah lah lah lah lah lah

eye could not see it where - ev - er might be it, The
sweet - er and dear - er by far when 'tis bring - ing The
lah lah lah lah lah lah lah

D.C. v. 2
dim.
p
bark that is bear - ing my lov - er to me.
bark of my true love in safe - ty to me.
dim.
p
lah lah lah lah
D.C. v. 2

9. The Miller's Flowers

Translated by
Arthur Langford

Franz Schubert
(1797-1828)

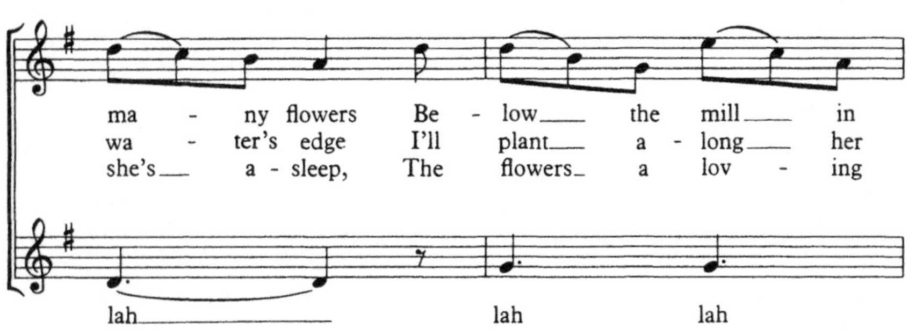

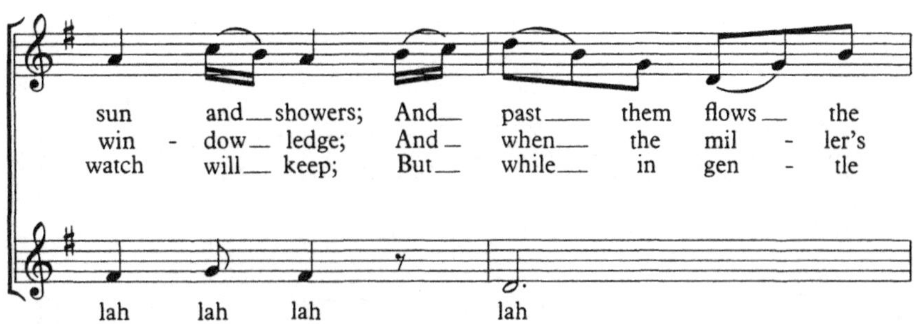

The words are reprinted by permission

murm - 'ring stream Whose wa - ters in the
daugh - ter fair Leans out to breathe the
sleep she lies, They'll nev - er close their
lah lah lah
mp
sun - light gleam. These are my
sum - mer air, Sure - ly she'll
own blue eyes, For they are
mp
lah lah lah lah
p
own for - get - me - nots, These are my
then for - get me not, Sure - ly she'll
my for - get - me - nots, For they are
p
lah lah lah lah lah
1&2 D.S. vv. 2, 3 3
own for - get - me - nots.
then for - get me not.
my for - get - me - - nots.
1&2 D.S. vv. 2, 3 3
lah lah lah. lah.

10. Susanni

Carol in two parts

15th-century words

Old German tune
arranged by Fritz Jöde

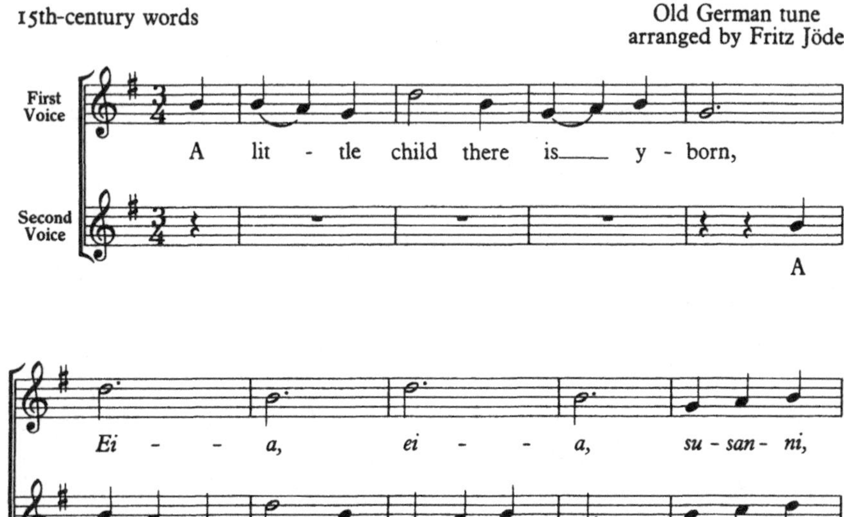

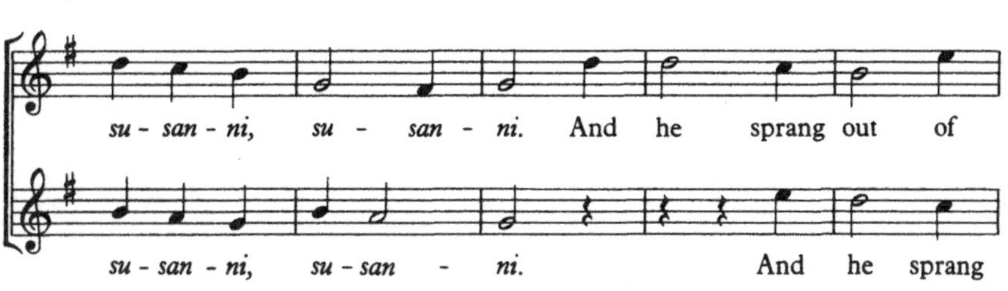

2. Now Jesus is the childès name,
   And Mary mild she is his dame;
   And so our sorrow is turned to game.

3. It fell upon the high midnight,
   The stars they shone both fair and bright,
   The angels sang with all their might.

4. Three kings there came with their presénts
   Of myrrh and gold and frankincense,
   As clerkès sing in their sequence.

5. Now sit we down upon our knee,
   And pray we to the Trinity,
   Our help, and succour for to be.

11. The Shepherd

Words by
William Blake

Harry Brook

hears the lambs' in - no - cent_ call,
And he
hears the lambs' in - no - cent_ call,
And he
poco rall.
pp
hears the ewes'_ ten - der re - ply;
He is
pp
hears_ the ewes'_ ten - der re - ply;
He is
pp
mf
watch - ful while_ they are in_ peace,
For they
pp
mf
watch - ful while_ they are in peace,
For they
rall.
più lento
p
know when their shep - herd_ is nigh.
How
p
know when their_ shep - herd_ is_ nigh. How sweet is the_
rall e dim.
sweet is the_ shep - herd's sweet_ lot!
shep - herd's sweet_ lot!_ How_ sweet!

12. Song of the Spirits

from 'Armide'

Words by
Jacqueline Froom

Gluck (1714-1787)
Edited and arranged by
W. G. Whittaker

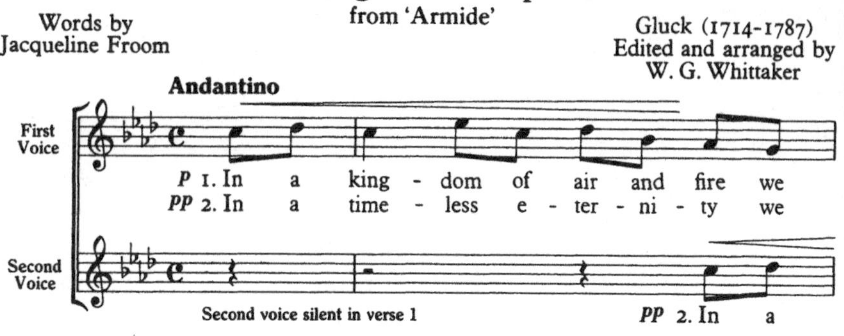

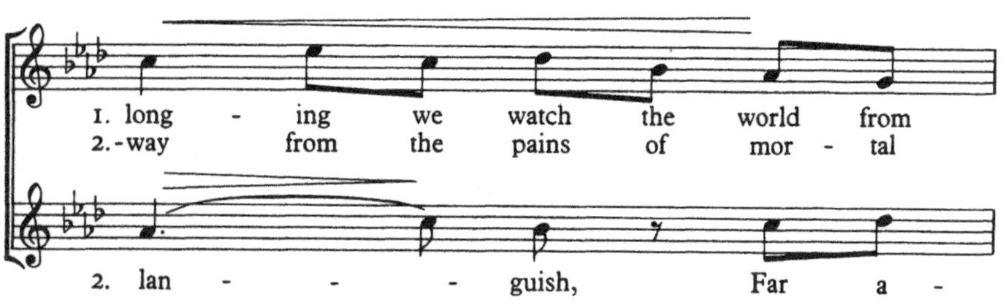

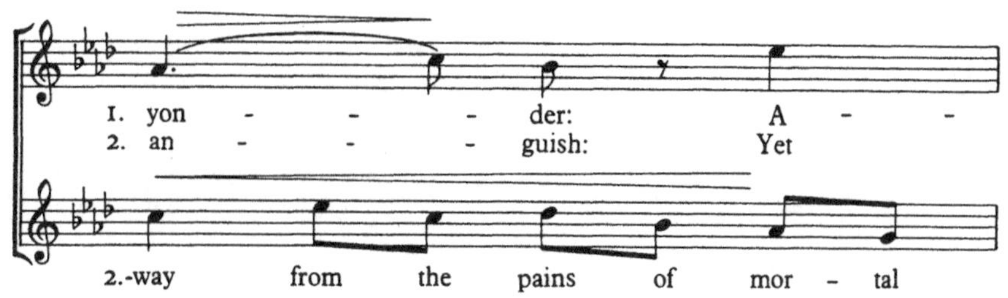

1. -las! from the earth ne - ver free.
2. still our dear home - land we see.
2. an - guish: our home - land we see.
CHORUS (to be sung by both voices in both verses)
p cresc.
Life! Thou must let us go! How -
p cresc.
Life! Thou must let us go! How -
mf
p
- ev - er we re - gret, O free_ us from be -
mf
p
- ev - er we re - gret, O free_ us from be -
cresc.
mf
cresc.
- low: The world we_ must for - get._ Hea - ven's_
cresc.
mf
cresc.
- low: The world we must for - get. Hea - ven's_
f
D.C. v. 2
gates o - pen_ wide And we must there a - bide._
f
D.C. v. 2
gates o - pen_ wide And we must there a - bide.

13. Oh, wha's for Scotland and Charlie?

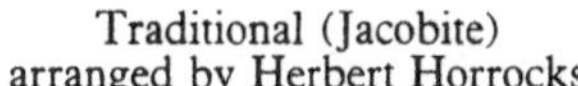
Traditional (Jacobite)
arranged by Herbert Horrocks

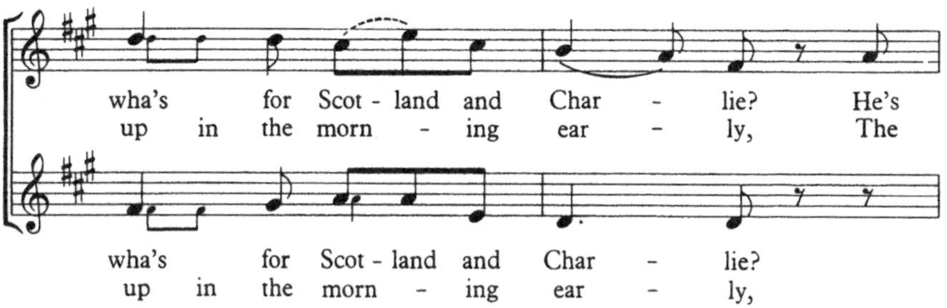

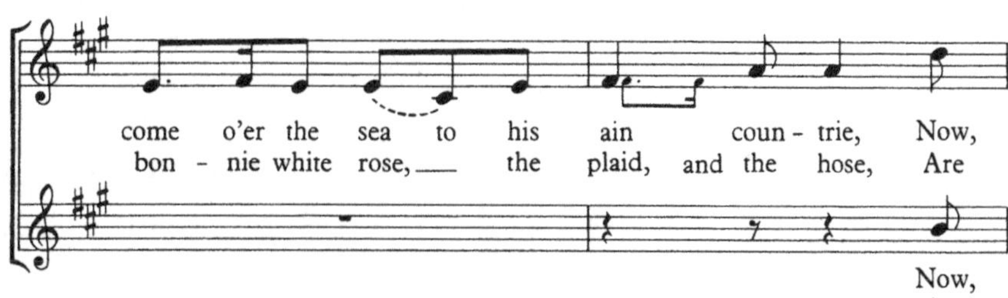

★Awa', auld carlie, = away old fellow.
★★Whaur ye've been sae lang = where you've been so long.

14. Sweet Kate

she, Glad - ly would I
she, Make no fool of
Glad - ly would I see
Make no fool of me!
see A - ny man to die with_ lo - -
me! Men I know have oaths at_ plea - -
A - ny man to die with lo - - -
Men I know have oaths at plea - - -
mp
- ving. Nev - er a - ny
- sure. But their hopes at -
- ving. Nev - er a - ny yet
- sure. But their hopes at - tained,
yet Died of such a fit, Nei - ther have I
- tained, They be - wray they feigned, And their oaths are
Died of such a fit, Nei - ther have I fear of
They be - wray they feigned, And their oaths are kept at
D.C. v. 2
fear of_ pro - - - ving.
kept at_ lei - - - sure.
pro - - - - - ving.
lei - - - - - sure.

15. Summer

(Air from 'Alcina')

Words by Jacqueline Froom

Handel (1685-1759)

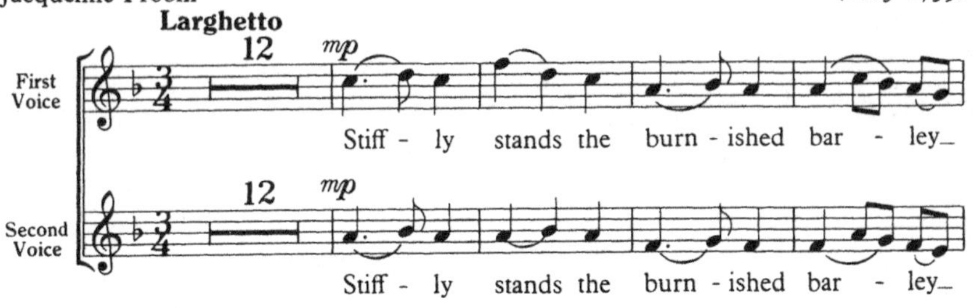

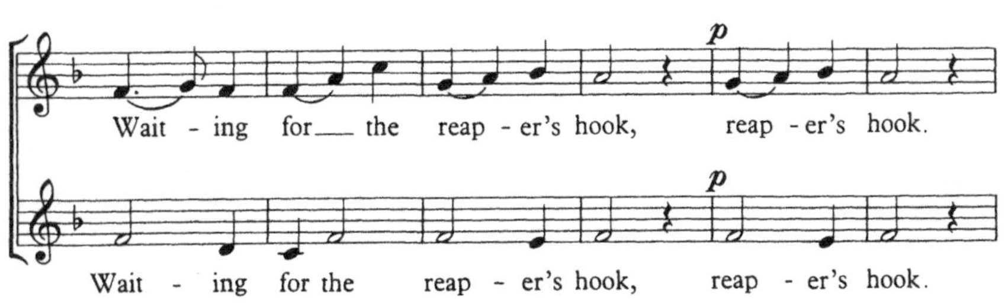

p
2
mp
brook, la - zy brook. See how shrun - ken
p
2
mp
brook, la - zy brook. See how shrun - ken
mp
are the dew-ponds, Cracked the earth and dry the leaves.
mp
are the dew-ponds, Cracked the earth and dry the leaves.
mf
mp
Is the sum - mer ne - ver end - ing? Ga - ther in the
mf
mp
Is the sum - mer ne - ver end-ing? Ga - ther in the
p
pp
gol - den sheaves! Gol - den sheaves! Gol - den sheaves!
p
pp
gol - den sheaves! Gol - den sheaves! Gol - den sheaves!
4
mf
4
Ga - ther in the gol - den sheaves!
4
mf
4
Ga - ther in the gol - den sheaves!

16. How merrily we live

Michael Este
(c. 1580-c. 1648)

f
sing with mer - ry glee, Roun-de - lays still we
f
sing with mer - ry glee, Roun-de - lays still we
Fine
1
2
p
sing with mer - ry glee. glee. On the plea-sant downs, where
1 Fine 2
p
sing with mer-ry glee. glee. On the plea-sant downs, where
f
as our flocks we see, On the plea-sant downs, where
f
as our flocks we see, On the plea-sant downs, where
p
as our flocks we see, We feel no
p
as our flocks we see, We feel no
f
p
cares, we fear not for - tune's frowns, We
f
p
cares, we fear not, fear not for - tune's frowns, We

feel no cares, we fear not for - tune's
feel no cares, we fear not, fear not for - tune's
f
frowns; We have no en - vy, which sweet
f
frowns; We have no en - vy, we have no en - vy, which sweet
p
mirth, sweet mirth, sweet mirth con - founds, sweet mirth con -
p
mirth, sweet mirth, sweet mirth con - founds, sweet mirth con -
- founds, con - founds,
- founds, We have no en - vy, which sweet mirth, sweet mirth con -
Adagio
D.C. without repeat
We have no en - vy, which sweet mirth con - founds.
D.C. without repeat
- founds, We have no en - vy, which sweet mirth con - founds.

17. The Loadstars

Words adapted from Shakespeare

William Shield (1748-1829)

mp
shep-herd's ear. O hap - py, hap - py, hap - py, hap - py
mp
shep-herd's ear. O hap - py, hap - py
fair,_ Your eyes are load-stars, and your tongue sweet air.
fair,_ are load-stars, and your tongue sweet air.
mf
More tune - a - ble than lark_ to shep - herd's_ ear,
mf
More
to shep - herd's ear, When
tune - a - ble than lark_ to shep - herd's ear,_ When
wheat is green, when haw-thorn buds ap - pear, When wheat is
wheat is green, when haw-thorn buds ap - pear, When wheat is

p
mp
green, when haw-thorn buds ap - pear, More tune - a - ble than
p
mp
green, when haw-thorn buds ap - pear, More
lark, When wheat is green, More
tune - a - ble than lark to shep-herd's ear, More
mf
tune - a - ble than lark to shep-herd's ear, When wheat is
tune - a - ble than lark to shep-herd's ear,
mp
green, when haw-thorn buds ap - pear; O hap-py, hap-py,
mf
p
mp
when haw - thorn buds ap - pear; O O
hap - py, hap - py fair, Your eyes are load-stars, and your
hap - py, hap - py fair, are load-stars, and your

tongue sweet air; hap - py fair, hap - py fair,
tongue sweet air; hap - py, hap - py,
cresc.
hap - py, hap - py fair, Your eyes are load - stars, your
cresc.
hap - py fair, Your eyes are
dim.
eyes are load - stars, your eyes are load-stars, and your
dim.
load - stars, your eyes are load-stars, and your tongue
cresc.
tongue sweet air; Your eyes are load -stars, your eyes are
cresc.
sweet air; Your eyes are load -stars, your
f
load - stars, your eyes are load-stars, and your tongue sweet air.
f
eyes are load- stars, are load-stars, and your tongue sweet air.

18. Ho-la-hi

Translated by
Roger Fiske

German folk-song
arranged by Roger Fiske

cresc.
ho - la - ho, What my true love's name can be,
cresc.
ho - la - ho, What my true love's name can be,
f
Ho - la - hi - a - ho. Let them won - der,
f
Ho - la - hi - a - ho. Let them won - der,
mp
let them tease, Ho - la - hi, ho - la - ho,
mp
let them tease, Ho - la - hi, ho - la - ho,
f
mp
I shall love just as I please, Ho - la - hi - a -
f
mp
I shall love just as I please, Ho - la - hi - a -
non rit.
4
2
- ho.
non rit.
4
2
mp ma marcato
- ho.
Spite - ful peo - ple

f — *p* *f* — *p*

Ho - la - hi, ho - la - ho.

f — *p* *f* — *p*

some - times hiss, Ho - la - hi, ho - la - ho.

mf

Ho - la - hi - a -

mp *mf*

"No - thing good can come of this," Ho - la - hi - a -

mp *cresc.*

- ho. "She will ne - ver_ be your own," Ho - la -

mp *cresc.*

- ho. "She will ne - ver_ be your own," Ho - la -

mf cresc.

- hi, ho - la - ho, Yet do I love_ her a -

mf cresc.

- hi, ho - la - ho, Yet do I love_ her a -

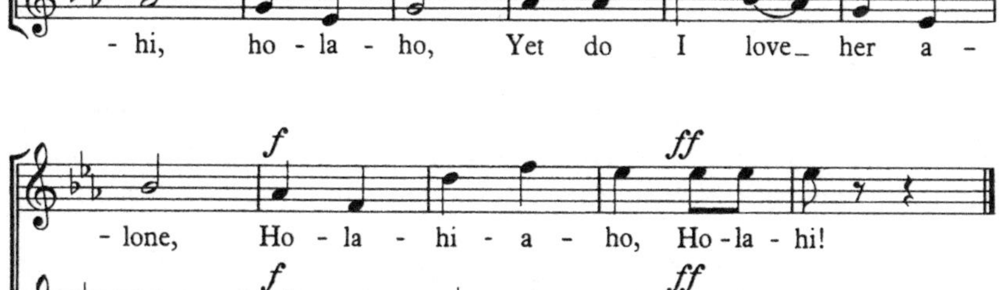

Firsts and Seconds

19. Song of farewell

Words by
Ursula Vaughan Williams

*Austrian folk-song
Collected by Engel Lund
Arranged by Ferdinand Rauter

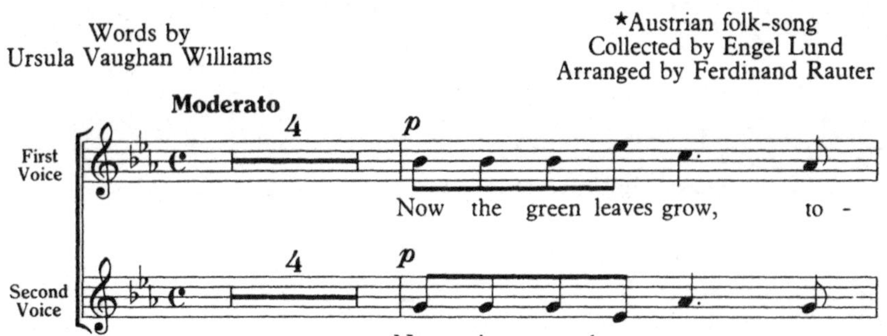

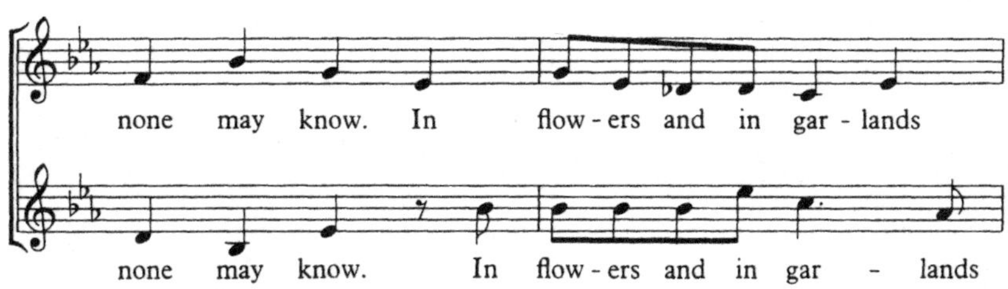

*From *A Second Book of Folk-songs* by Engel Lund (O.U.P.)

go — a - way. This must be my fare-well, I
go a - way. This must be my fare-well, I
will not come a - gain, Nor
will not come a - gain, Nor
shall I leave a foot - print, light as
shall I leave a foot - print, light as
snow or rain. Friends I must for - get,
snow — or — rain. Friends I must for - get, O
think of me — and say A
think of me and say A

mf
pa - ter nos - ter at the end of day. A -
pa - ter nos - ter for me at the end of day.
- men, a - men, a - men. Your words will stand and keep Their
mf
A - men, a - men. Your words will stand and
watch and guard a - round me where I sleep. A -
p
p
guard a - round me where I sleep. A -
- men, a - men. Your words will stand and keep Their
- men, a - men, a - men. Your words will stand and keep Their
watch and guard a - round me where I sleep.
watch and guard a - round me where I sleep.

20. Li'l David play on yo' harp

Negro Spiritual
arranged by Sebastian H. Brown

Hal - le - lu.
play on yo' harp, Hal - le - lu.
mf
1. Da - vid was a shep - herd boy, He kill Go -
2. Josh - u' was de son ob Nun, He ne'er would
- li'h an' shout fo' joy.
quit till work be done.
Da - vid was a
Josh - u' was de
shep - herd boy, He kill Go - li'h an'
son ob Nun, He ne'er would quit till
(Li'l Da - vid play on yo' harp), He kill an'
(Li'l Da - vid play on yo' harp), He ne'er would
dim. molto

2
(clap hands)
D.S. v. 2
shout fo' joy.
work be done.
2
(clap hands)
D.S. v. 2
shout fo' joy.
quit till done.
pp
Li'l Da - vid play on yo' harp, Hal - le -
pp
Li'l Da - vid play on yo' harp, Hal - le - lu,
rall.
a tempo
- lu, Li'l Da - vid play on yo' harp, Hal - le - lu.
Li'l Da - vid play on yo' harp, Hal - le - lu.
p
Li'l Da - vid play on yo' harp,
p
Li'l Da - vid play on yo'
mf
f
Hal - le - lu, Hal - le - lu.
f
harp, Hal - le - lu.

21. Cielito Lindo

Words by
Jacqueline Froom

Mexican folk-tune
arranged by Phyllis Tate

★Pronounced "See*ay*-lee-to"

Firsts and Seconds

OXFORD UNIVERSITY PRESS